J. B. Kelly, I.M.C.

Christopher Columbus

A Buddy Book
by
Christy DeVillier

Publishing Company

VISIT US AT

www.abdopub.com

Published by ABDO Publishing Company, 4940 Viking Drive, Edina, Minnesota 55435.
Copyright © 2001 by Abdo Consulting Group, Inc. International copyrights reserved in all countries. No part of this book may be reproduced in any form without written permission from the publisher.

Printed in the United States.

Edited by: Michael P. Goecke
Contributing Editor: Matt Ray
Image Research: Deborah Coldiron, Susan Will
Graphic Design: Jane Halbert
Cover Photograph: courtesy of Library of Congress, Washington, D.C.
Interior Photographs/Illustrations: pages 8, 9, 14 & 23: courtesy of Library of Congress, Washington, D.C.; page 4: courtesy of The Mariners' Museum, Newport News, VA; pages 5, 27, & 28: Deborah Coldiron; pages 15 & 24: North Wind Picture Archives; pages 21 & 25: Denise Esner; page 22: Maria Hosley

Library of Congress Cataloging-in-Publication Data

Devillier, Christy, 1971-
    Christopher Columbus / Christy Devillier.
       p. cm. — (First biographies)
    Includes index.
    ISBN 1-57765-594-X
    1. Columbus, Christopher—Juvenile literature. 2. Explorers—America—Biography—Juvenile literature. 3. Explorers—Spain—Biography—Juvenile literature. 4. America—Discovery and exploration—Spanish—Juvenile literature. [1. Columbus, Christopher. 2. Explorers. 3. America—Discovery and exploration—Spanish.] I. Title.

E111 .D48 2001
970.01'5'092—dc21
[B]

                                        2001022298

Table Of Contents

Why Is He Famous?

Christopher Columbus

Christopher Columbus was a famous explorer. He lived in the 1400's in Europe. Italy, Spain, England, Germany, and many other countries are in Europe.

Back then, many Europeans explored the world. They liked to find new land. People already lived on much of this land. So, this land was only new to the Europeans. Columbus is one of these European explorers.

Explorers used tools like this eyeglass and compass.

Christopher Columbus is one of the first Europeans to find South America. He also found many islands in the Caribbean Sea. Some of these islands are the Bahamas, Cuba, Hispaniola, Jamaica, and Puerto Rico.

These places were like a "New World" to Europeans in the 1400's.

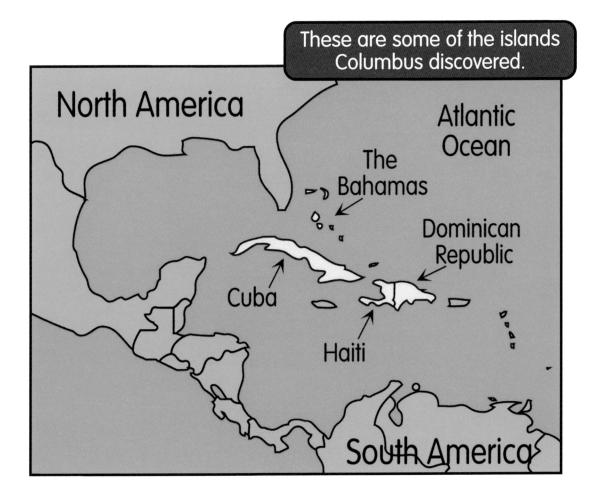

These are some of the islands Columbus discovered.

North America

Atlantic Ocean

The Bahamas

Dominican Republic

Cuba

Haiti

South America

Growing Up

Christopher Columbus

Christopher Columbus was born in 1451 in Genoa. Genoa is in northern Italy. Young Christopher did not go to school very much. Yet, he taught himself to speak Portuguese, Spanish, and Latin.

Christopher was interested in the sea. He spent time at Genoa's busy port. He sailed on trading ships in the Mediterranean Sea.

Young Christopher sailed on trading ships.

First Steps

In the 1470's, Christopher Columbus moved to Portugal. There, he worked on Portuguese ships. Columbus learned about sailing in the Atlantic Ocean on these trips, or voyages. He learned how to navigate a ship at sea, too.

Columbus moved from Italy to Portugal.

In 1479, Christopher Columbus married Felipa Perestello e Moniz. They had one son, Diego.

Columbus read about Marco Polo. Marco Polo was a famous explorer. Marco Polo had found gold and other riches in the Indies. Columbus wanted to find this land of riches.

Christopher Columbus wanted to sail to the Indies in a new way. This new way was sailing west across the Atlantic Ocean. Columbus thought this way would be faster.

Finding Help

Sailing to the Indies cost a lot of money. Christopher Columbus did not have enough money. He needed help.

Columbus asked King John of Portugal to help him. King John said no.

Columbus asked the king and queen of Spain for help.

Next, Columbus asked King Ferdinand and Queen Isabella of Spain. At the time, Spain was in the middle of war. So, they did not give Columbus any money until 1492.

Christopher Columbus's Ships

In May 1492, Columbus found ships for the big voyage. He found three ships at the port of Palos in Spain. These ships were trading ships.

Columbus found ships at the port of Palos.

The Niña, the Pinta, and the Santa María were trading ships.

Two of these ships were light and fast. These ships were the Niña and the Pinta.

The third ship was larger and slower. It was the Santa María. The Santa María was Columbus's flagship.

Preparing For A Great Voyage

Next, Christopher Columbus needed a crew for the voyage. This could have been very difficult. Many people were afraid of sailing in the Atlantic Ocean.

In the 1400's, people did not know much about the Atlantic Ocean. They did not know how big it was. They did not know if someone could sail across it. They believed the Atlantic Ocean was full of sea monsters.

The Pinzón brothers helped Columbus find a crew.

Columbus found two brave men, Martin and Vicente Pinzón. They were brothers. They agreed to captain the Niña and the Pinta. They helped Columbus find a crew. The crew was made up of 90 men and boys.

It took 10 weeks to get everything ready for Christopher's great voyage. They loaded the ships with enough food to last a year. Also, they packed tools, weapons, and other supplies. Columbus and his fleet set sail on August 3, 1492.

Columbus spent 10 weeks preparing for the great voyage.

The First Voyage

Sailing in the 1400's was not easy. The ships were small. The crew had to sleep outside on the deck. There was no extra water for bathing. The crew wore the same clothes every day. Fleas and lice were a problem. The crew was often bored and in a bad mood.

Many days passed. No land was in sight. The sailers worried about getting home.

On October 12, 1492, someone on the Pinta spotted land. Columbus named this first island San Salvador.

Columbus found the New World in 1492.

The Taino lived on San Salvador.

Columbus and his crew found people living on San Salvador. They welcomed Columbus and his men. The islanders called themselves the Taino. Taino means "good people."

Columbus thought he had reached the Indies. But he was wrong. He was not even close to the Indies.

This is how the Europeans
thought the world looked.

Columbus thought the Indies were
closer to Europe. Still, he found many
lands new to the Europeans.

On October 28, 1492, Columbus found
a big island. We call this island Cuba.

Columbus thought he had reached the Indies.

Then, they sailed to another island. Columbus called this island La Isla Española, or Hispaniola. Hispaniola was full of gold and other riches. Today, the countries of Haiti and Dominican Republic are on Hispaniola.

Welcome Home

In 1493, Christopher Columbus returned to Spain. He brought gifts to King Ferdinand and Queen Isabella. He brought back six islanders, parrots, and gold.

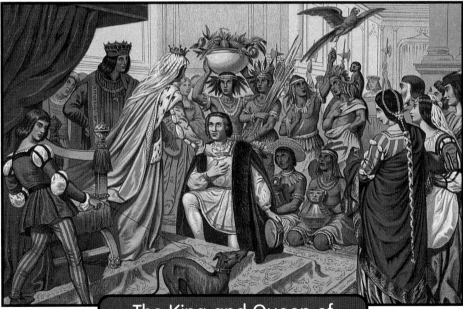

The King and Queen of Spain welcomed Columbus.

Columbus presenting the King and Queen with gifts.

King Ferdinand and Queen Isabella were happy with these gifts. They called Christopher Columbus "Admiral of the Ocean Sea."

More Voyages

In September 1493, Christopher Columbus sailed back to Hispaniola. This time, he had a fleet of 17 ships. Columbus brought supplies to make a Spanish settlement on this island.

The Spanish built a settlement on Hispaniola.

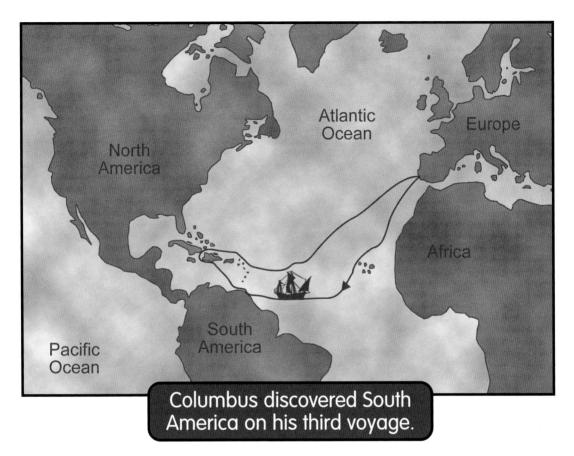

Columbus discovered South America on his third voyage.

Columbus sailed across the Atlantic two more times. He found South America on his third voyage. This is why we say Christopher Columbus discovered America.

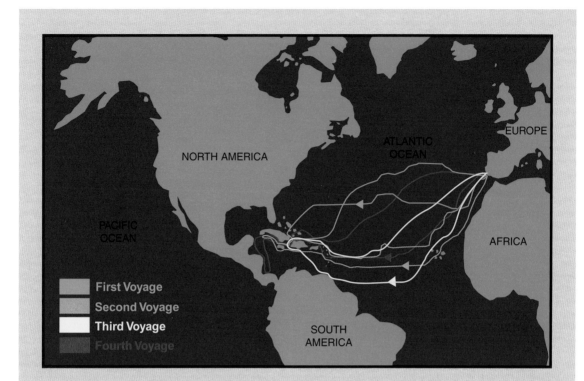

CHRISTOPHER COLUMBUS'S VOYAGES

First voyage, 1492–1493:
San Salvador (Bahamas), Cuba, Hispaniola

Second voyage, 1493–1494:
Antiqua, Dominica, Guadeloupe, Jamaica, Puerto Rico

Third voyage, 1498–1500:
Grenada, Margarita, St. Vincent, Trinidad, Venezuela

Fourth voyage, 1502–1504:
Costa Rica, Honduras, Martinique, Nicaragua, Panama, St. Lucia

Columbus Day

Christopher Columbus was a good sailer. He could navigate his ship from place to place very well. Columbus was a brave man, too. He was not afraid of the great Atlantic Ocean.

Today, we remember Christopher Columbus by celebrating Columbus Day. Columbus Day is on the second Monday of October.

Columbus Day

Important Dates

1451 Christopher Columbus is born.

1484 Christopher Columbus asks King John of Portugal to sponsor a trip to the Indies.

1492 King Ferdinand and Queen Isabella of Spain give Christopher Columbus money.

August 3, 1492 Christopher Columbus and his crew set sail across the Atlantic Ocean.

October 12, 1492 Christopher Columbus and his crew spot land. They have discovered the New World!

October 28, 1492 Columbus discovers Cuba.

December 5, 1492 Columbus discovers Hispaniola.

September 1493 Christopher Columbus begins a second voyage to the New World.

May 30, 1498 Christopher Columbus begins a third voyage with six ships.

Summer 1498 Columbus finds South America.

May 11, 1502 Christopher Columbus begins his last voyage to the New World.

Important Words

crew a group of people who work on a ship.

explorer someone who searches for new land.

flagship the ship that the leader or captain rides on.

fleet a group of ships.

navigate to find your way from place to place.

New World what people called the western part of the world in the 1400's.

port the place where ships load or drop off goods.

settlement a village.

Web Sites

The Columbus Navigation Homepage
http://www1.minn.net/~keithp/
This site examines the history, navigation, and landfall of Christopher Columbus.

The Explorations of Christopher Columbus
http://www.mariner.org/age/columbus.html
Each of Columbus's four voyages are mapped and described here.

Index

J. B. Kelly, I. M. C.